21

Highly Effective Productivity Hacks for Work from Home

Managing your work effectively and productively

Startup's Dictionary

CONTAINS

Getting Started

When COVID-19 happened, most of the people were forced to either shift their work or shut their work completely! Maybe you have found the dream job where you can work-from-home or, Maybe depending on the current situation, your work has shifted to work from home. Either way, It is not an easy task. Work from home comes in with many challenges of its own. BUT no matter what, you need to accept and move forward with it. You need to learn how you can adapt yourself and get things done as well within the set deadline. Working remotely has many benefits. Some of the basic ones being: It reduces your time commuting, getting ready for work, It gives you more flexible hours, etc.

But despite that, it's challenging. Working from home carries its own set of unique challenges. It takes dedication and Effectively laid out systems to pull it off successfully. And here is what most people struggle to achieve. life and vice versa. If you are not careful enough, soon, it gets very difficult to draw the line.

These challenges are not just limited to work, but even balancing your home life. When you work from home, your workspace and your personal space are intertwined. By the time you learn to balance your work, your personal life a mess, and when you try to balance that out your work life will be a mess. Your personal life becomes your work life and vice versa. If you are not careful enough, soon, it gets very difficult to draw the line.

Now, to maintain a healthy lifestyle, it is highly recommended to look and make changes in how we work and manage our life. Especially now more than ever! Not just because of the type of work we do. Learning to balance your life and work is now a priority to have a healthy lifestyle. Right now if Work from home is all-new for you. You have never worked from home in your life and you've always used to having an office, co-worker, or boss that you're accountable to.

Now, when you have no one looking over your shoulder or structuring your day, it becomes all too easy to fall prey to bad habits. A 5 minutes break can turn into an hour of distracting activities. Or you can just get lazy to do your work. It is so important to gain the exact mindset that can help you tackle this type of challenge in the best way possible Every home-based worker deals with different types of challenges, depending on their circumstance. They have to figure out when to work, where to work, how to set goals and achieve those goals. The most difficult struggle above all is how to set up the boundary between your personal life and work life. But, many of the primary issues they face are the same. In this book, we will discuss the most useful productivity tips that work best and you will also learn what are the things which drain out our productivity and how to avoid them.

Setting up the Mind-set:

Working from home is all about having the right mind-set. It's about shifting the way you think about work, and how you train yourself to be able to operate with an incredible focus. Most people believe that productivity while working from home is a myth. So, is work from home productivity a fact or fiction? Well, according to research, work from home has shown increased productivity as an equivalent to a full day's work. Compared to a full day's work in office workers. A home-based worker takes shorter breaks and fewer sick leave. Also, it saved a lot of time from commuting to the office. Being an in-office worker takes a lot of discipline. You need to dress right. Be on time to commute and other challenges. This book is aimed to help you manage work from home more efficiently and successfully.

#1 - Plan your Day

The first one and probably one of the essential tips to start is to make sure you plan out your day. Ideally, plan out your weeks and then plan out your every week daily. This way, you have a plan for every day of the week. Planning can make you proactive throughout the day, NOT reactive.

Suppose you fail to plan out for the day. You can easily fit into someone else's plan. The challenge arises when a lot of people don't have a plan. They have no idea what they are supposed to do. They just jump into whatever is handed over to them. By not having a definite plan for the day, they don't have a purpose for what they want to do that day.

So they start the day by opening up the computer. They check their email. They check their social media. They check their messages; they check their phone. And now they're spending the first part of the day just reacting to everyone else.

You are just responding to everyone's demands everyone else's urgencies of what they need from you. You're responding to them, and yes, you're reacting now and helping them out. But what's happening is that you're missing out on what you got to be doing.

You're missing out on doing the most important and the highest leverage actions that are going to move YOUR needle and make the most significant difference in your work or your job and so having a structured plan is paramount for being proactive.

So, before you even open your computer or before you even sit down for work. Take out a journal/ Planner or open up Evernote or any app that you have on your computer or phone that can help you plan. Create a plan for that day. First, start with:

What do you want from this day?

What do you want to accomplish today?

What are your goals?

What is the intention you have?

List out every task and goals you have in your mind once it's out as a list. Now you have a more transparent view of things you need to do. The next step is to create a plan.

The next thing you need to do is, ask yourself, which task from the list you need to do,

The task that can help you move closer to your goal?

Ask yourself, what is that everything that I could do to achieve this goal on this day?

What can you do today to achieve this outcome?

Then create a to-do list in order of your task.

Now, this doesn't have to mean that you do everything on that one day.

The main objective of this activity is to give you an overview of the actions that you need to take.

Once you have that list of actions, the next important step is to prioritize that list. Which means out of everything that you have to do, which task has to be dealt with first, which of the listed job are of the utmost priority.

Say if you have ten things that you want to do for that day. You need to understand that not everything there is equal. Not all activities, not all actions are equal, as they don't produce an equal outcome. This is the stage you need to decide which of the following action can make a huge difference or move you closer to your goal. Not all of those actions are going to lead to bigger results. Some actions which seem small may give a bigger reward than others. Some of them are going to move the needle even more than others. It's called 80/20 principles that the 20% that is on your list is going to equal 80% of the results.

This is where most people struggle with. It's not with time management; it can prioritize what is more important on that list.

Identify what is most important in your list and then make sure that it is the number one thing that you do for that day. So, once you are done making your list, planning it out, then make sure to schedule it on your calendar. Schedule and block the time for all the tasks that you will be doing at that particular time.

#2 - Start your day early

One of the great and not-so-great things about work from home is that your time is flexible. It's great because you can work whenever you what to. Not so great because you work when you have to.

When you are working in an office is so happens that you have a morning routine. You wake up and start your day which is mostly spent on getting ready and commuting to the office. But, while you work from home. Making yourself to wake up, and sit for work can be challenging.
When you have an office that you go to, you try to wake up on time. Get ready for work on time and you try leaving your house on time so you could reach your office on time. Now, a lot of these activities are eliminated when you're at home. You mostly wake up late and get your work started late.
The beauty of working in an office is that you get to leave the house and go to work every single day. This is rhythmic, it's automatic, it's just what you do. Unfortunately when you start working from home that routine goes away.
Which is by the way now, a dangerous thing, because now you have slower starts and longer finishes.

Work from home is no doubt freedom. Freedom to be your own time. But, this freedom also means procrastination, laziness, and being unproductive. Sometimes you may feel busy, but busy on the wrong things.

One of the best ways to stay productive while working from home is to wake up early and dive into your to-do list as soon as you are up, first thing in the morning.

Simply getting started first thing in the morning can be the key to making progress. Because when you try to delay your morning, you tend to prolong the breakfast and let that morning sluggishness wear away your motivation for work. When you delay working first thing in the morning you tend to fall prey to things like. " oh, I'm' too tired". " Let me watch an episode on Netflix." " Let me start work an hour later." "It is still working from home right? I can work whenever I want to." - All these things will slow you down. They make you lethargic and you tend to delay your work further. you are never getting into the mood for work.

Get into a morning routine ASAP:
So, even when you don't have to clock in-to work each day, still try to make yourself used to a morning routine.

A morning routine can help you jump-start your day and in many ways, it will help set yourself up for a very productive day.

That means setting an alarm and getting up at the same time each day. That means take that shower, make that pot of morning coffee or tea whatever. Do whatever you need to do, to get your day started the right way.

Also, it helps if you could change into regular clothes, not on your PJs. or just change out of the pajamas that you are in. That ritual of changing out of what you were sleeping in and getting out of that pajamas can transform your mood significantly. Now, this doesn't mean you need to put on a suit and tie every day.

This routine helps you get that kick start you need to work. It motivates you and helps you establish your work timeline. Morning Routine and productivity go hand in hand.

If you establish and stick to a morning routine, you can quickly get back into a productive rhythm that prepares your mind for the work ahead each morning.

#3- Setting up your office space

Now, a lot of people who happen to start working from home for the first time are surprised to find that their home life and their work-life kind of meld together.

But, the reason that happens is pretty obvious. These activities are happing in the same space. So the way to mitigate that is also obvious. Try to create some dedicated space where you do your work.

Create a designated work area:
As tempting as it might be to work from your bed or living room recliner, creating a designated work area that at least resembles the type of space you are used to working from is sure to make you much more productive. We are impacted heavily by our environments, and an environment meant for rest and leisure doesn't always lend itself to maximum productivity.

Yes, you may feel you would be much comfortable working on the couch or sitting on your bed. In comparison, these places for sure provide you comfort. They also increase your desire to relax.

Instead, try to create an environment at home that is meant for work and productivity.

So, the first step you need to take to create a designated work area is to find your spot.

Choose a room or a spot in your home where you can be with the least distraction. That is away from the TV, kitchen, or the kid's playrooms.
Make sure you have all the necessary office tools before you sit down to work. You shouldn't constantly be getting up to get a paper or pen etc.

Now, a home office is a pinnacle, if you can have a home office- is fantastic! But, a lot of people don't have that luxury. So, if you aren't able to have a home office, see if you can get a desk. Even if it is a small desk that can fit into your bedroom where you can primarily set up as your workspace. This space creates a mental separation between work and home.
Now, once you have set up the workspace, don't just stop at investing in the ergonomics; also consider investing in the aesthetics of your dedicated workspace. Like you can think about color, texture, plants, art, all of these things can make the experience of working in your workspace far more pleasant or anything that can make you happy to work. Some motivational posters, to-do list. Etc.

#4 - Act like in the office

A lot of new home-based job workers find it difficult to get out of their work mood because both your work life and your personal life are now overlapping each other.
This makes it hard to draw the line. You would feel you are always at work. 24 hours a day. You end up spending so much time worrying about your work even when you are not working.
 Your life activities take a hit.
Now the beauty of a 9 to 5 job. That at 5 pm, no matter what, you're done for the day, so you mentally check out of work, which gets very hard to do when you're working from home. Even though you are at home, you feel you are attached to work all the time.
When a dedicated space becomes your regular spot, so when you go in, you mentally check-in for work and get things done. On the flip side, when you get up and get out of there or leave that space, you can mentally check out of work.
When you mentally try to associate your workspace with your office. You can check-in for work and check out of the place to be out of work. Balancing your personal and professional life becomes much more manageable.

#5 -Work your regular hours

 Few things that are going to help you be more productive while working from home is that sticking to your regular schedule. This means that you schedule and structure your day like you are in the office. Working like you would during in-office hours.

These are the hours that your mind and body have become accustomed to working over the years, and they are the hours when you are sure to be most productive.
While a lot will change your workday if you start to work from home for the first time, one thing that can remain the same is the hours you are on the clock.
 Keeping this vital detail, the same as it has always been, will go a long way towards keeping you as productive as possible while working from home as you would be if you were working from the office.

Now, this not only helps you to work when you should be work. This can also help you not to work when you shouldn't be working.

#6 - Beware of the temptation to work when you shouldn't

When you start working from home, it so happens that you get so involved in your work that you forget to take a break from it. Even when you are not working, you will be thinking about work.

This happens because your work life is now overlapped with your personal life. Not just physically, but mentally too. The boundary between your work and your personal life gets thinner and thinner each day.

In this situation, you no longer work from home; it becomes more like you have a home where you work. This gets even worst for your relationships.

You no longer give your time to them. Even when you do, you are not there for them mentally because you are always thinking about work.

You are always thinking about your next move, the next project, or even the next email you will write.

You forget to live in the moments. You get stuck in work, mentally, even if you are not physically.

Working physically and mentally when you shouldn't. That would be a disaster for relationships either with your partner or even with your kids. This not only affects your personal life; this also drains your overall energy levels both physically and mentally. You no longer spend your time during the activities that you love, just as you are supposed to know when you should be working. Know that you should also set a time when you shouldn't be working.

Set yourself a login and log out time and don't overwork than you should be. Turn off all work-related notifications when you are off work. Schedule and make sure you block a set of times just for You. Block the set of time to do the things you love. Go out, walking, swimming, and even watch a movie while you eat popcorn. Give yourself a break and to those around you. Spend some time with your loved ones. Make some calls to your friends. Try to enjoy life for what it is. It doesn't always have to work.

7 - Know what you are supposed to be doing

Time is precious. Let's not waste it. Imagine you take an 8 hr a day and shrink it down to 6 and still able to get some things done. By being more efficient and productive in handling your work.

When you are set to work, let's make sure that you are working on the things that matter, when you think about it while you are working from home and your work doesn't require you to check-in and checks out of hours to make sure that you get your stuff done.

When you sit down and start with your work, you try to deal with the urgent matter first in hand, by the time you are done with it. You just jump into the most straightforward task next.

There is no denying that working from home takes a lot of effort. You will be trying to do a lot of things at hand. You're doing emails, vision planning, working on presentations, project reports, and so on and on. You realize there is just so much work to do. But, you also need to understand is that there is only so much work you CAN DO.

Now the trick is to understand which of those things are going to help you the most. Which of these tasks is going to help you move forward?

Which of these tasks can help you move forward in your job? But the problem arises when we have dealt with the urgent things, we end up doing what the easiest or the work we are most comfortable with. These tasks aren't the things that move the needle for you. They may push you forward incrementally, and they sure can make you feel busy. But, honestly, you know that the things that move you more are the things that are a little bit more uncomfortable. These are are the things that you procrastinate with.

Identify your tasks: have a running list of all the things that you need to be doing. When you don't have it, you will not know what to do. Once when the list is made. Go down the line one by one to see which ones are the most important in terms of moving you forward in your work, not just keeping you busy. Then when you do have that, make sure that you are working on the ones who are moving the needle first.

#8 - Schedule all parts of your day

Your calendar is sort of your best friend in this situation when you are working from home. You probably have your meetings already in your schedule, but some essential things should be placed in too. Like, your morning routine and all things you will be doing for the day.

No! This doesn't mean you have to schedule when you are going to put coffee into the mug and when you are going to be out of the shower. You don't have to get into that detail of the tasks. Just put in the block of time when your morning routine starts. Block on the calendar the time you will be working on different tasks for the day.

This way, you can systematically follow the things you have to be doing. So, when you look at the calendar, you will know what exactly you should be doing and how much time you will be spending on that particular task. Get into a habit to regularly schedule your tasks.

"If it doesn't get scheduled, it doesn't get done."

It is essential that you also schedule your breaks. Again when you don't put them in there, they are not going to happen.

Next, you want to schedule when your check out time is. This will be your version of 9 to 5 pm.

Maybe you have a long working day, and have a specific end time is the key to create those boundaries.

Maybe you split your work hours into various chunks during the day. Even then the end of each of those chunks, you can help yourself by mentally checking it out. Seeing on the calendar and even notifying yourself even when the time comes around.

Plus, knowing that when you are starting something, there is no endpoint to it, well you can't help but want to be efficient to maximize that time for yourself.

#9- Being Flexible

Now, if you have kids at home or someone who needs your attention now and then. You need to remain flexible with your working hours. Scheduling every part of your day can act as a guideline. For which you can decide that these are the hours to try and focus on work. Get things done those big-ticket items. But, being flexible is the key.

Sometimes things may not go as well as they should. Some tasks may take up a little extra of your time, or you might get interrupted in between your work.

There can be a break in your workflow state, and mentally it is going to be quite tough, especially when you're used to remaining in those hours and only used to do things in those hours.

But, now that you're in a different environment you have, kids, you have other distractions, your spouse or your parents. You need to understand that you will be interrupted every once in a while. So, when you schedule all parts of your day, make sure you leave a little extra block of time, maybe towards the end of the day or before your break to make up for the things you missed.

Working from home is all about balancing what you are supposed to be doing when you are supposed to be doing, and when you shouldn't be doing it.

And yes, you have the freedom to be flexible on how you work things out.

10

Proactively identify and mitigate any distractions you encountered during the day

When you're working from home, you are surrounded by all of the activities you usually do during your free time. When you're not in an office, you don't have coworkers around you to provide additional accountability to stay focused on your task. So, you have to take up the slack and make sure that you're mindful and present and paying attention to how those distractions are affecting your performance during the day.

Is having the Television on really helping you in your productivity?

Are you checking your phone more than you usually would?

How many trips have you made in the last two hours?

All these sorts of distractions can keep you from doing your best and most productive work. So, pay attention to the things that are distracting your workflow. Be humble and honest to find how those distractions are affecting you.

Eliminating distractions is very important. If you've other people in your house, your family, your kids, when your working close the door, put a sign on the door, let people know that from this time to this time it's your working hours. So, when the door is closed, do not enter.

You need to set these boundaries. Not just Physical boundaries also Digital Boundaries - it is very easy to answer phone calls; it is very easy to respond to text messages. It is very easy to check your Facebook or youtube or email inbox. You might be compelled to check your social media now and then. Whatever it might be, those are all distractions. And they're taking you away from doing the important things.

Make sure that you turn off your phone, turn off anything that would distract you from doing what you have to be doing. Some people try to Navigate through these distractions by Multitasking.
When you multitask, you are trying to do all these different things, and you're constantly distracted by so many tasks that you are doing. This is going to lower your ability to focus on one core thing.

Always keep your focus on one task at a time. When you focus on one core activity, you get into the flow state, which is a state that is the peak of productivity.

Every interruption and distraction which pulls you away from your flow. It takes about 20 mins for the brain to go back into that state, into that zone of flow. This is the reason why multitasking is never really the way for productivity.

#11 - Peak State

Manage your emotional state:
Make sure that you are in your peak state before you start your day. Your emotional state dictates your behavior. How you feel, your emotions are going to determine your performance.
A lot of people don't have a routine before they start their workday. If you take a look at any professional athlete or any top performer before they go out and perform, they want to make sure that they are at their best. So they have a routine that they follow that prepares them for the day.

Let's take an example of Cricket players or any players, they have a routine before the game. They stretch to warm up their body. Meditate to help them focus and calm their mind. They all have their very own routine they follow to make sure they can perform at their max potential.

It's the same thing for you too for every day of your work. Spending just a few mins beforehand to make sure that you're feeling good, energized, motivated, and inspired can help you get more confident and focused in your work.
So, have a routine that can help you get into a peak state. Maybe a little exercise or meditation, reading a book,

affirmations whatever that can get you to turn on your mind, and feel supercharged. All those things that make sure that you are physically and mentally at your best!

#12 - Eat the frog:

What does that mean?
That simply means that out of everything that you got for
that day, you want to spend your first part of the day by
working on the most important and the highest leverage task
that you need to do for that day.

The reason why you need to do that early in the day is that
often our willpower wears out. If you leave a task, which is
essential to be dealt with for the later part of the day. You
end up having less willpower to do the task.

We have the highest willpower first thing in the morning. But,
as the day goes on, it gets depleted. That's why often when
you come home from work, and you're tired after a long busy
day. It feels a lot easier for you just to eat junk food, or sit
around on the couch and not be productive because you
have less willpower. It's a lot harder for you to get yourself to
go to the gym or workout and do certain things because you
have less willpower at that time. So that's why you need to
do the most important task first.
By doing that, you will be spending your most valuable time
and energy on a task that is going to make a massive
difference for you.

So eat the frog first thing, the most important thing to do. Do not delay, do not procrastinate with that.

#13 - Having a Deadline

Setting Deadlines:
When we implement deadlines into our tasks, it creates a sense of urgency, and the speed of finishing the task increases.
A lot of people are not productive because they work too slow. They don't set a deadline for themself to finish the tasks. They just take their time working away at things, and they can spend hours doing something that can be done in a few mins. Just like Parkinson's Law states:
"Work expands to fill the time available for its completion."

Whenever you start working on something, be it a small task or a long-term project set a realistic deadline for completion. Creating a deadline will create a sense of urgency, which is going to help you stay more focused and faster at your work.

#14 - Having a System

Find and organize a system that works for your personal life and professional life: It is really important to make sure that both aspects of your life are as organized as possible. Because if one is disorganized, the other one is going to feel disorganized as well. One of the biggest distractions that you encounter when you start working from home is that all the other things that you have to do.

It can be doing laundry or getting groceries, or maybe you forgot to send that email or return a call. You get nagged continuously with so many thoughts throughout the day. When you have a reliable organization system, this can allow you to take those thoughts off your mind and put it into an organization system so that it happens at the right time, not just because you thought of it.

When you think of a task, write it down as a note. This way, that thought is out of your head and will be dealt with at the right time.

The important thing is that when both areas are organized, you don't experience distractions. You feel overwhelmed or anything else which can bring down your productivity as a result of too many things to do and not knowing where they fit in your life.

#15 - Take breaks:

Taking breaks may seem like an enemy of being productive, but the reality is that a short break can refresh your mind and lead to more productivity in the end. While it is great that you are pushing yourself to be as productive as possible while working from home, it's essential to keep in mind that occasional breaks are the friend of productivity rather than its enemy.

Taking a break - mental breaks, physical breaks that get you outside, and move away from your work environment will help you come back even stronger.

Even when you are cranking on a deadline, this may seem hard, but just walk away from that just for a moment can help you re-energize and come back more focused and motivated. Just like cramming for a test, you would be better off taking a little break every once a while to re-energize.

Your break can be just a 10 to 15 min walk or a water break. Maybe even a nap. Taking a mental break from the work you are doing every once in a while can distract you from your stress and help you calm down.

#16 - Stay connected

Even if staying connected with your colleagues is not an absolute requirement for your job- which, in many cases, it will be - it's still a good idea to keep in touch with them and stay up-to-date on their progress. While also keeping them up-to-date on yours. You shouldn't let distance throw a wrench in your productivity when there are so many great video conferencing and collaboration tools available today. Staying connected while you work from home is sure to help you get more work done, and the good news is staying connected without communicating in-person is now easier than ever before.

Schedule a meeting with your colleagues from time to time to discuss work and progress. Try not to overdo it. Having a meeting three times a day just to discuss work is not going to move the work forward. Keep your meetings short and to the point. This not only helps you to stay informed about everyone. These opportunities build your relationships with the people that you work with and make you memorable, visible, and valuable.

#17 - Guard your work-life balance

The two big traps that work from home workers often fall into is allowing work to permeate their personal life to the point where there never really feels like there's a separation and the second one is being so fearful of not being visible or being perceived as slacking off that you don't take breaks. Lunches and vacations and you don't respect your working hours. It is really important not to fall into those traps. Take breaks, take lunch breaks, take vacations. Respect your work hours. When you're on, you're on, and when you're off, you're off. Now, there some jobs that require a bit of flexibility. You might be at a level professionally where being on-call is just part of your job. There's nothing wrong with that. But that doesn't mean that you need to be on and responsive 100% of the time the same way that you would be during standard working hours. Make sure to protect your work/life balance.

Have a scheduled and dedicated time with your loved ones, your family, friends. Spending time with them is so important and by scheduling time just for them, helps you check out of work and check in with them. This will ensure that when you do check out of work, you are fully available for them—both mentally and physically.

You want to be 100% with them during that time of the day. This also ensures that they know that once you are done with your work, you are going be 100% be with them later in the day. In that case, they are less likely to interrupt. Communicate about your working hours as much as possible with those around you.

#18 - Talk About Expectations

Talk to your roommates/ housemates about expectations. It doesn't matter what you're living situation is if it involves other people. You should probably have a conversation with them about what reasonable expectations are. A lot of times, if you live with people who don't have experience working remotely. They might make the mistake of expecting you to be available during work hours the way you are during the evenings and at the weekends.

During your work hours, your work is your number one priority the same way it would be if you were working in an office.
 Now, if you don't have this sort of conversation, you will probably end up in a situation where someone you live with asks you to do something or demands, your time in a way that you aren't able to fulfill. This can create conflict, and that conflict is avoidable by going upfront and having that conversation about expectations.
Especially with your loved ones or partners so you both can come to an understanding of your working hours. Because if you just create the schedule yourself and then don't share it with others, then that's not fair to the other people too. It can

benefit you to have the other person know when you should be in work mode. But, also, it can help them to know which time of the day you're going to be checking out so you can check in mentally with them.

If this is new for you, you are going to have to have a meeting to tell each other what the expectations are. Communicate about your time with your spouse or partners or roommates or even with your kids. The worst thing you can do is not communicate anything at all.

#19 - Managing Stress

Your mental health comes first!
Suppose you are overwhelmed with a lot of things going on in your life or work. You might feel less productive and frustrated.
You are not alone! A recent study has found that 75% of us are feeling less productive or feel overwhelmed, and working from home is not helping. It is full of distractions. Kids, pets, or anybody interrupting.
It is tough to take care of yourself when you are just feeling chaotic and isolated.
It becomes so important now more than ever to prioritize self-care. Taking care of your mental and physical health will not only help you, but it also strikes a balance between responsibility to others and responsibility to yourself.

Take a break to get a perspective:
When you are continually working and feeling overwhelmed about your work or a task, it can become difficult to focus, and gets easy to lose sight of the purpose.

Researches tell us that we do need to step away from always working. This will allow you to look at things from a broader perspective, which helps you to ensure that you haven't lost sight of the big picture.

Hitting that reset button by pulling away and pausing will allow us to access the one thing that we can control, which is our perspective.

Remember you cut yourself, in your brain some slack: During the period of ongoing stress. Our brain is wired to shut down that logical thought process and move into reactive mode, which is never a great idea. So, just be kind to yourself, remember it's your neurobiology to be kind to yourself and give yourself a break.

Don't forget to track and celebrate your progress: It is easy to get caught up in the crazy momentum and chaos of the time and forget that you've moved the needle. You need to track that either in a journal or just somewhere and use that at the end of the day, or end of the week to remind yourself how far you have come and feel more productive. When you are working from home for months, it's easy to feel you are not making progress, and you're super unproductive. But, you're not alone.

#20 - Choose to eat right

Now that you are not working IN the office anymore. There isn't going to be a dedicated time for lunch and breaks. When you are at work, it's easy for you to walk down to the office cafeteria and eat food that is readily available to you. You wouldn't have enough time to shift for a health option food. It was hard to keep an eye on your calorie intake and the nutrition you need. You easily fall prey to eat junk food and call it a cheat day. But now that you are at home working remotely, you have the freedom and the option to choose a healthier diet. Make sure you include short breaks in-between your work. Never try to skip your meal. Eating on time and healthy will improve your overall energy. Your body and mind will appreciate it. Your work will show it, so make those wise choices regarding your food and also make sure that you drink lots of water. Keep a glass near your work table, which will remind you to drink water from time to time. Try to take in light meals which can help you stay alert during work and as well provide you enough energy boost to get through the day.

Try to avoid heavy meals as much as possible during your work hours. Heavy food makes you feel tired and lethargic. As your eating habits directly affect the energy levels, so make sure you are taking in some healthy food that'll keep you pepped up all day. This makes a huge difference in your productivity.

Here is a list of foods that can keep your energies and active throughout the day.

Whole Grain Bread:

Try switching your diet to whole grain bread. It is a rich source of fiber, vitamin E, and B complex that give you sustained energy, which in turn provides you long-lasting energy. Have it at brunch or breakfast will help you will feel less sluggish.

Kiwi:

Have a kiwi smoothie and or a kiwifruit salad cab ward off that sleepy feeling. Kiwifruit is an essential ingredient that helps you in being active as its rich in copper and vitamin C.

Flax Seeds:

Adding flax seeds to your daily diet will strengthen your immunity and help in energy production.

Berries:

Berries are known to be a rich source of antioxidants, fiber, and vitamins that keeps you physically and mentally active throughout the day. An extremely nutritious food, berries have very few calories.

Protein Bar:

When you are feeling tired, grab a protein bar! It is one of the best ways to curb that sleepiness during the working hours, and they provide you with an instant energy boost. You can have it as a snack in between your meals.

#21 - Reward yourself

Always reward yourself at the end of the day for being productive.
Whatever gets rewarded gets repeated. Subconsciously you feel good about yourself for all the productive work you did for the day.

Whenever you had a great productive day and when you reward yourself, you're more likely to build your habits into the future, and you get better and better and better.
You can have a set up for the day of all the things you wanted to do and enjoy. It can be done later in the day as a reward for being productive. Say you want to watch your favorite Netflix series. Or you want to spend your time with loved ones, family, and friends to connect and do those things that are indulgences that are pleasurable for you.
That's the reward for a productive day.